Thirty
Go to th

ex libris

Candlestick Press

Published by:

Candlestick Press,
Diversity House, 72 Nottingham Road, Arnold, Nottingham UK NG5 6LF
www.candlestickpress.co.uk

Design and typesetting by Diversity Creative Marketing Solutions Ltd.,
www.diversity.agency

Printed by Ratcliff & Roper Print Group, Nottinghamshire, UK

Poems © George Szirtes, 2018

Illustrations © Natalie d'Arbeloff, 2018 www.nataliedarbeloff.com

Candlestick Press monogram © Barbara Shaw, 2008

© Candlestick Press, 2018

ISBN 978 1 907598 61 6

Acknowledgements:

We would like to thank Martin Figura for his kind permission to publish
'George Szirtes Goes to the Gym' within this collection.

Contents

Basho Goes to the Gym   7

John Berryman Goes to the Gym   8

John Betjeman Goes to the Gym   9

Elizabeth Bishop Goes to the Gym   10

William Blake Goes to the Gym   11

Elizabeth Barrett Browning Goes to the Gym   12

Lord Byron in the Guise of Don Juan Goes to the Gym   13

ee cummings goes to the gym   14

Dante Alighieri Goes to the Gym   15

Emily Dickinson Goes to the Gym   16

John Donne Goes to the Gym   17

TS Eliot Visits the Gym   18

George Herbert Goes to the Gym   20

Philip Larkin Goes to the Gym   21

William McGonagall Goes to the Gym   22

Marianne Moore Goes to the Gymnasium   23

Sylvia Plath Goes to the Gym   24

Alexander Pope Goes to the Gym   25

Ezra Pound Goes to the Gym   26

Rainer Maria Rilke Goes to the Gym   27

John Wilmot, 2nd Earl of Rochester   *28*
Goes to the Gym

Theodor Roethke Goes to the Gym   *29*

Edith Sitwell Goes to the Gym   *30*

Stevie Smith Goes to the Gym   *31*

Wallace Stevens Goes to the Gym   *32*

Gertrude Stein Goes to the Gym   *34*

Dylan Thomas Goes to the Gym   *35*

François Villon Goes to the Gym   *36*

Walt Whitman Goes to the Gym   *37*

William Butler Yeats Goes to the Gym   *38*

Coda

George Szirtes   *Martin Figura*   *40*
Goes to the Gym

'Mens sana in corpore sano'

Basho Goes to the Gym

The moon is high
A drop of sweat falls
Plop

John Berryman Goes to the Gym

Unfit Henry considered his options
& stript down to his essentials
& swung his barbells in circular manner
arms fully extended. Hey Mr Bones
what wif de pecs? Of Henry's
sadness is no ending, sighed Henry

and melancholy is bad news as ever
& the whisky & paprika
& the star-swallowing ambition of Henry
is a fault, but Henry will run &
run on dat belt, until his belly
subside under his curtain of beard

and be lean and magníficent
and of service wif ladies & in
the night time build his body into Henry
& his dreams. Sez you, Mr Bones?
Is true Henry? True & not true Mr Bones.
I is Mr Muscles now, beardless.

John Betjeman Goes to the Gym

Adorable and twice as slim
As I who labour in the gym
Your muscles solid, derrière
Hard as a hardwood bentwood chair,
With wristband, hairband, dressed to kill,
Kill me, with barbells, if you will.
> *Kill me with barbells, crush my toes,*
> *Break the assurance of my nose,*
> *Assume your Amazonian pose,*
> *But love me when the gym doors close.*

Shopping in Willesden, bruised by rain,
I think of your beauty once again,
Down Dollis Hill, along the tube,
My fingers crushing my Oxo cube,
I'm back in the gym, I'm lifting plates
While all the while my huntress waits.
> *Kill me with arrows, burn my prose,*
> *Lord, how I pray we may come to blows,*
> *But love me when the gym doors close.*
> *Dear, love me when the gym doors close.*

Elizabeth Bishop Goes to the Gym

The art of walking isn't hard to figure;
so many creatures walk and stay upright
that uprightness seems just a form of rigour.

Keep walking. Use the treadmill, walk with vigour,
walk faster, longer, walk right out of sight.
The art of walking isn't hard to figure.

Then practise striding stronger, striding bigger;
you've walked down streets and seen people alight
from buses. None of these requires much rigour.

I once tripped over. I made people snigger
and still survived embarrassment and fright.
The art of walking isn't hard to figure.

I kept on tripping, tripping was the trigger
for more disasters, yet remained polite
since uprightness seemed just a form of rigour.

Even tripping over your toy digger
the one you kept from childhood isn't quite
an art like walking that seems hard to figure
though it may look like lack of (sod it!) rigour.

William Blake Goes to the Gym

Then Theotormon did from the press arise and speak
to gentle Oothoon. Thou labourest at the mill and treadest
the machines of fiery Bromion in the Vale of Leutha
where flowers spring before the golden shrine
of beauty. But wherefore in the gymnasiums of Albion
doth Oothoon weep and languish? Art thou a weakling?

No thou art a cry in the throat of Bromion as his feet pound
the orbit of the sun. Arise then, Oothoon in swift delight
from the satanic mill and fly to the rower pulling against
the tides to follow an impetuous course. Then thou,
like Milton will resume the crest with furious energies
that bide not in the shower rooms of Reason…

Elizabeth Barrett Browning Goes to the Gym

How do I pound thee? Let me catch my breath.
I pound thee like a horse, a herd, a horde
Of buffalo until I'm sick and bored
And sore exhausted, almost to my death.
I tread thee every day and will unless
My trainer relent and I am thus restored
To that condition which man might afford
Through years of strife with treader, bench and press.
I pound thee purely, as a child at prayer
Addressing God, and passionate as dawn
In all its fervour in that stifled air,
Or as a startled rabbit on the lawn
That pounds and scurries in its wild despair,
And so unto the treader am I drawn
To meet my fate and for my Lord prepare.

Lord Byron in the Guise of Don Juan Goes to the Gym

Mens sana in corpore sano. Perhaps.
It is an idea not now much propounded
(We tend to keep our Latin under wraps
These days in case we old Harrovians sounded
Like one of those truly dreadful Eton craps
Like Jake Rees-Mogg whose poshness is unbounded).
Where was I? Yes of course! I sing of health
Which is man's prime concern (that's after wealth).

For me, I boxed and wrestled, wenched and drank.
(My wenches were occasionally male
For which I have biographers to thank,
Whose views of one eventually prevail.)
My private gym was half passion, half prank,
Though nothing bores me more than pranks gone stale.
I hate all exercise that's repetition.
Variety has been my life's whole mission.

But I digress. My figure kept quite well
Providing I maintained a dietary austerity
Of hock and soda water for a spell
Followed by feasting. There's no parity
Between a blow-out and a prison cell
But a change is as good as a rest (that verity
Might qualify as a truism, that's true,
But I rather like the odd cliché or two).

No bench-press or treadmill in my home equipment.
I did possess an ancient vaulting horse
That I received from Venice in a shipment
Though I far preferred the real thing of course.
(I have fond memories of what a trip meant
Back then, of love and sex without remorse.
My love affairs were not with rails and rings.
They were with flesh and feast, such finer things.)

e e cummings goes to the gym

L(oo)k here is a hand-
                    WEIGHT

  Raise it above your HeaD

breathe (BREATHE)   (breathe)   breathe

  now drop

        IT

(but gently so-o-o it does not hurt your **f**(look!)**t**

OUCCCH!

  Try "*!!*" again

Dante Alighieri Goes to the Gym

Midway this path of life we're bound upon
I came upon a door on which was written
This message: *Spirit and body are one!*

Your soul may yet be saved though it be smitten
With forms of sin yet to be classified,
But you must pay the fee to be let in.

What is this place? I ventured of my guide
And he to me: This is the place of trial
Where bodies are trimmed clear of mortal pride.

Within the door there queue the tragic file
Of such as have neglected trunk and limb,
Those mighty engines ranged along the aisle

Are means whereby the glutton may grow slim.
Then one addressed me from his seat of pain.
I who was fat am doomed to years of gym,

Nor must I ever eat cream cake again
Until my purgatorial time is finished.
With that he turned, returning to his bane.

I see, I said, how mortal sin is punished.
With monstrous puffing and with pools of sweat,
Nor is the pain relieved or once diminished.

Take heed, my guide advised. There's more pain yet.

Emily Dickinson Goes to the Gym

I heard a car start – in the yard –
As I was Pedalling –
The Great Machine turned at my feet –
My Trainer signalling.

I clutched my Kitbag – but the Sun
Caught me in the Eye –
No one pedals in Paradise
The thought upon me grew –

And then the car – moved past the Glass
Turned round – and swiftly left.
There was no Paradise in View –
And I remained – bereft –

My Body moved – as if on fire –
And Breath was coming fast
For that last Effort – when the Sun
Entered – like a Fist –

John Donne Goes to the Gym

Since we are met above this instrument
Whose wheels look to revolve and yet do not
It seemeth me the time that heaven lent
Is as a circle moving on a spot
And when the circle closes we are lost,
Our sky in disarray, our stars uncrossed.

Behold my heart that poundeth all too fast
From spinning with thee in that desp'rate sphere
That though it race is sure to finish last
And when you end still remaineth here.
So am I left with shadows of the tape
Thou breakest, being of the fitter shape.

Why should we then keep turning in our rounds
And pedalling for all that we are worth
When thou hast covered far remoter grounds
Than I have voyaged in my time on earth.
My eyes are seas that weep against the shore
Unless thou stopp'st and we rotate once more.

TS Eliot Visits the Gym

And so each visit
Is a new beginning, a raid on the inoperative
With shabby equipment, never good as new:
The treadmill whose plain discourse often falters,
The pedals that betray the pumping foot.

O Vishnu in the boiling cataract!
Shantih at the flood, O three white leopards
Would you do better in such circumstance?

Tristan and Jojo
Rowing hard
Pulling steady at the oars
Watching their heartrate
Increasing their pace
Brows furrowed
Muscles pumping
Outside the car-park
With the eternal sound of rain.

Weilala, Princess Leia,
Weilala, Jackie

And you who raise the weights tonight at sundown,
And you who trudge on the eternal mill
Consider Jackie who was fat as you

Burning burning

Time gentlemen, please, it's time.

Auf Wiedersehen pet
Arma et virumque cano
La plume de ma tante est dans le jardin

Unreal

Goodnight gymnasts, good night sweet gymnasts
Goodnight Jojo, goodnight Jackie,
Good night, good night.

And it's O O O O
O my bloody back!

George Herbert Goes to the Gym

Indeed, O Lord, Thou didst for us devise
A proper stature and true weight
In belly and in thighs
Fit for our state
And size.
But soon,
In greed and sloth,
Began man to balloon
And blow till he, alas, was loth
To stir at all but once in a blue moon.

Then didst Thou create that Mighty Dome
By which a man might be defined
If he yet cared to come
In prayer to find
His home.
And there
Where bench and press
Are as sacrament and prayer
Didst Thou, in Thy great Tenderness
First tread the mill and our weight-loss prepare.

Philip Larkin Goes to the Gym

I work all day and lift barbells at night
Waking to find myself prostrate on the floor,
Exhausted, dizzy, always mildly tight,
Then slope off vaguely lurching for the door
Beyond which waits the dark street and the house
Where I curse and wank myself into a drowse
To rise dishevelled in the morning after
With library books strewn across my desk
A sad case of grotesque
Fitted for death and chock-full of sour laughter.

What is it for? There's no purpose in this.
It's Coventry followed by bloody Hull
With Belfast as a brief parenthesis.
The years are all too short and deadly dull.
What's work? A sack of toads. Across the park
Toads squat and leer into the winter dark.
I ride my bike and hold on to my hat
Drifting through the suburbs like a ghost.
Life's one bike at the most,
Its gears inoperative, tyres flat.

So back to the gym. My biceps and my thighs
Are still developing though not too far.
It is my specs that win the Nobel Prize.
It is my raincoat in the glittering car.
I tread the treadmill all the way to Leeds
And back to Hull as lure of sex recedes
Into the twilight. Now I raise the weight
And hold it steady as the gym doors close
And night-time turn to prose.
I must be heading off now. It is late.

William McGonagall Goes to the Gym

O magnificent gymnasium of Wymondham Leisure Centre
That is, aye, a pleasure and of great benefit to enter
For since I started there in Two-Thousand and Seventeen
I have felt better than I have ever been.
The lockers are abundant and the showers
Are hot so people stand in them for many happy hours,
And the tread-mill moves at such governable pace
That no man there will fall off them backwards, sideways or forwards, aye, flat
                 on his face,
Which makes the people of Wymondham safer and fitter
And shows how it is indubitably better to be a walker than a sitter.

Marianne Moore Goes to the Gymnasium

I too dislike it with its
apparatus of absolute clarity
in face of a physical body that articulates
the geometry of hoist and crane as well as of
the bulldozer against which the frail
tendon and neuron, and fribble of carpals
(scaphoid, lunate, triquetral, pisiform) –
is likely to come off second best.

So paraphernalia of belt and weight and barbell
present an opposition, a kind of what-is-this of
hand and wrist, with the corresponding
muscles of the arm and shoulder moving
in traction.
This,
one might venture, is beauty
or at least capable of a presentation of such ambition –
observed, as if from outside the gymnasium,
looking in.

Sylvia Plath Goes to the Gym

You do not do, you do not do,
Any more, gym shoe
You fascist pig,
With insole full of goo.
My toes are black and blue.
And who do I blame? Yes, you.

Daddy, I have had to dump you
before your time was through.
Your bloody laces like a noose
Just one left so no use
Although I once had two.

Your Nazi heels,
Your terrible pooh-pooh,
You tortured me
But now I torture you
I pommel and pommel you.

With all your stitching torn,
With your flailing Polish tongue
And your tread full of dry dung.
You'll wish you'd never been born
By the time that I am through.

Ach, ach, ach, ach
You fascist bastard you…

Alexander Pope Goes to the Gym

And now, unveil'd, the Treader stands display'd
Not least in the Immaculate Parade
Of Apparatus the keen Eye absorbs
Along with Beams and Bars and Rods and Orbs
At which Belinda gives a haughty glance
As local Sparks still push, press, pull and prance,
Belinda, half divine, whom all Adore
Whene'er she crosses the Gymnasium Floor,
For whom a Host of love-bedizened Swains
Bestir themselves to most Peculiar Pains,
Continues with her conscious Term of Toil
And so their Hopes and Passions daily Spoil.
Not Pride alone but thought of Health compels
The Goddess to partake of Bikes and Bells
Wherefore Belinda to her Labour bends
And sets her legs to work to serve her Ends...

Ezra Pound Goes to the Gym

Yeau taught men to do sit ups
  and attend upon the low bike
having magnificent legs on which to stand
            in the old days

McGarrie sat at the pianola strummin'
  Dové la maetropolitana. Parla piano per favour.

Them's mighty tough folk, thus Borommeo who ran away to Florence

Tarda una hora en conocerte y solo un dia en enamorarme.
Pero me llevará toda una vida poder olvidarte
            a touch of Provençal

 and thou shalt not escape nor pay dues unto the usurers
for there is no longer brick laid upon brick *in maniera gymnastica*

罐

dat's cat on a hot tin roof for yez

龍

and Kung raising weights by the river.
        'There were gymnasiums by the old temple and men exercised,'
remarked Yuan Jang
  homerta in Sicily is a man rowing nowhere fast, said Kung

        Banish *usura!* (Benito 1927)

I will build my body, replied Kung.

Adieussiatz commendatore. See yez later.

  Then was gone with the rains.

Rainer Maria Rilke Goes to the Gym

Sometimes you hear a cry as of a bird
Or a strong angel and a violin start
On the corner, such as you once heard
In a forgotten street of your mind's heart,
And you think of bodies striding apparatus
As you might well have done had you but listened
To their singing and known the full afflatus
Of the stars where all the windows glistened
With your childhood, and so you entered in
And paid your fee and learned to run or row
With your whole body, breathing through your skin.
You transcendental creature! Where will you go
To be yourself? And will you still be fit
Next year? Says spirit: You must change your kit.

John Wilmot, 2nd Earl of Rochester Goes to the Gym

All that exertion, passion gone to ****
Have I, quoth he, but visited for this?
Is rowing forth a cure to make man sick
And lose the function of exhausted *****?
And how does that serve any woman's want,
** **** and ******** to *** ****
Or truly please the languishing Atossa
By turning from Adonis to a ******?
Too much of exercise, we lose the lust,
So that which should be iron turns to rust.

Theodor Roethke Goes to the Gym

In moving slow he has no Peer.
His treadmill ever in low Gear
He trudges on from Year to Year.

Nil gradient, on Level One,
Disdaining every thought of Fun
He stays there till his time is Done.

His speed will never Dip nor Spike.
He never gets to ride the Bike.
It's 'What I like is what I like.'

He walks for ever in his Dreams.
He neither Grimaces nor Beams.
It's just the air before him Steams.

Edith Sitwell Goes to the Gym

Do not take a step on the trainer
Gaynor
On the holy Sabbath on a weekend day
For if you do you might have to pay
And that's the way you'll learn
To discern
That you, dear girl, have calories to burn.
So listen, Gaynor,
Is it not much saner
To steer clear of that foul cross-trainer?
It's such a no brainer for the spry,
Since there are countless other things to try.
Then all the bikes leapt in the air
And the old pro said
Give it space over there
Either to the side or overhead
For the bees in their bonnets
About curtal sonnets
Are taking over the gym
And their overweight octaves are far from slim
While as for the six that follow
They owe nothing to Apollo
Or the Muses nine
Lacking a meter for a decent line.
For none will dance nor prance nor fit well.
Without a senior salty Sitwell.

Stevie Smith Goes to the Gym

Nobody heard him the dead man
He seemed to be rowing.
I was only ever half way across, he said
And not coming but going.

Poor bloke, he always loved exercise,
And now he's clapped out,
Not exactly drowned but buggered all the same.
Why didn't he shout?

Oh no no no, I never have shouted
(He muttered while slowing).
I was half way up shit creek all of my life
And not coming but going.

Wallace Stevens Goes to the Gym

I
A barbell in a wood
Is a barbell. In a gym it is
Two barbells.

II
I saw a barbell on the floor
And raised it.
The wood lacked a barbell.

III
Over the distant mountain
The barbell is silent
And invisible
Yet is a barbell.

IV
What would you have me do?
Be a barbell in a wood
Or in a gym with the barbells
On the floor?

V
The barbell lay in the snow
With the bench-press
It was winter.
The gym was cold
Because the door was open.

VI
O barbells of the south
Had you been in the north I might have seen you
While I was lifting barbells
Singing yet silent
Strong yet underwhelming.

VII
A man in the yard
Found a barbell. The barbell was still.
The man was moving.
The mountains were silent
In the barbaric valley.

VIII
A song about a barbell
Is a song. A barbell without a song
Remains a barbell.

IX
Over in the woods the woodchucks
Were calling for barbells.
The emptiness of the woods
Was a denial of euphony and whirling equipages
In a rain of barbells.

X
In the gym there was
An orderly arrangement of barbells.
The crystals were tinkling
In Haddam among the scholars.
The bluebells were elsewhere
Talking of barbells.

XI
A man and woman in a gym
Are a man and women in the gym.
A barbell on the floor is a coincidence
In a world without barbells.

XII
The rejoicing of the barbells in the mountains
Is the delight of the woods under the mountains
Among the wild roses
The barbells are gathering.
The indifference of the barbells
Meets the indifference of the roses.

XIII
The barbell lay on the floor
Next to the man.
It must be evening.

Gertrude Stein Goes to the Gym

They went to the gymnasium. Their bodies required it. Their bodies were their requirements were their bodies and required it. They required it. They sat at machines and required it. Their bodies were sitting. Their bodies were standing. Sitting and standing were their bodies. The machines were the requirement of their bodies. Their legs walked, pedalled, walked. They walked. They pedalled. It was spring. Spring required it. It was the requirement. The gymnasium was the requirement. They pedalled. Their legs were moving. They kept pedalling. Pedalling and walking was what they required. Their bodies required it. Their bodies were at the machines. They were in the gymnasium. They were pedalling and walking at the machines. It was spring. Their bodies required it. Those were their bodies. Those were their requirements. They pedalled and walked. It was spring. Spring was required. The gymnasium was the gymnasium. It was spring in the gymnasium. The gymnasium was spring. They required a gymnasium. They required it.

Dylan Thomas Goes to the Gym

All the day long it was running, it was squatting, the rings
High as the ceiling, my earphones
Filled with the playlist
That was playing forever
And fit I was, drinking water and apple juice
The light through the window pounding and capering
Like goats or like sparrows or ferrets
And I was cowman and goatman and sparrow and ferret
Vaulting with the nightjars,
Golden and purple in the heydays high-days of youth.
Happy as Harry, spinning, brilliant, carefree and toned
As the universe in its mild cups...

    [Falls off the treadmill]

François Villon Goes to the Gym

Tell me where, in what far flung
Land is Perry who lost a stone,
Who was quite old but looked so young
Where has that strapping figure gone?
He used to exercise alone
And looked calm and could hold his beer,
His muscles were in perfect tone.
Where are the jocks of yesteryear?

And where are Buster and Dick Crabbe
Who ran for miles while keeping still?
And Gary with his layers of flab?
And Dave the bent, and show-off Bill?
Where's Stuart of the iron will
Who late was wont to disappear?
What of the boys that trod the mill?
Where are the jocks of yesteryear?

Big Alec who would whinge and fart
And used to stand at the home end,
Has gone for ever from the chart
He used to keep with Pete, his friend.
What then O Prince does this portend?
Why do the fit all disappear?
Why does the body never mend?
Where are the jocks of yesteryear?

Prince, the exercise is tough,
The nights too rigid and austere.
An hour a day is quite enough.
Where are the jocks of yesteryear?

Walt Whitman Goes to the Gym

I sing the body elastic and flexible
with a good deal of six-pack and bodily hair
as dense as the grass as I raise my chest proudly in proper tempo
for your chest is as my chest in the gymnasium and vice versa
as also at the bench press and the barbells on the bicycle machine
that crosses these great plains while standing firm
and I in the saddle pumping at the pedals
to drive us both forward.

Do I astonish, O my captain?
Does the early redstart twitter through the woods?

William Butler Yeats Goes to the Gym

Turning and turning on the parallel bars
The gymnast cannot hear beyond his breath;
The asymmetric bars lose symmetry;
Perspiring hands begin to lose their grip;
Too late the body in its quest for grace
Now the equipment's down and tocsins ring
Within the nerves. The gyres are all gone.
The fittest flounder, those who tread the mill
Approach their limits, no more pounds to shed.
Surely the dancer must become the dance.
Surely this is the hour the world awakes.
The world awakes! Hardly are those words out
When a vast image, vest and pyjama clad
Troubles my sight: somewhere in a house
A man-half-ape or ape-half-man appears
His belly enormous, swaying before him, trundling
Across the darkness, more gorilla than man,
With bloodshot eyes while all around him reel
Indignant gymnasts. Then the vision fades,
But now I know what physical perfection
And Olympic spirit lose in dreams.
And in that nightmare, what simian form
Slouches towards the bench-press to be born.

Coda

George Szirtes Goes to the Gym

There is a whole array of contraptions
all designed to inflict well-being
and mostly based on pedalled rotation.

I favour the Terza Rima Elliptical Running
Pro-Max Supreme, which is repetitious too
but has a pleasing progressive swing

to propel you forwards to the new you
one belt notch at a time. Muscle burn
is called for now, this isn't haiku

or even a sonnet, one must turn
a page and take care of what you eat:
stick to roots and leaves and Quorn,

poached fish perhaps, but no red meat,
chicken breast, shorn of skin and taste,
for a treat, a minuscule slice of fruit,

chocolate oranges don't count. Based
on research, at least half an hour of vigour
a day is needed. Clarissa sets the pace

so fast, like her paintings, she's a blur.
I am, I'm afraid a little less sprightly
carrying the burden that literature

brings – how to finish metaphorically
and disembark the machine with dignity?
Well, like a poem – step off lightly.

Martin Figura